Brilliant
RESILIENCE

Becky Dickinson
Illustrated by **Liz Kay**

OXFORD
UNIVERSITY PRESS

Letter from the Author

I hope you enjoy reading this book on resilience. More importantly, I hope it encourages you to follow your dreams, and to realize that making mistakes only makes you more brilliant.

When I'm not writing books or magazine articles, I love spending time outdoors, especially near the sea where I live, walking with my dog and three children, or trying to surf, which is great fun but takes quite a lot of resilience – especially when it's cold and I keep falling in!

I also love gardening and growing vegetables, although the slugs enjoy them too, so I am constantly looking for ways to outwit them. Fortunately, the results are worth it. I certainly find fresh air, mud and exercise make me feel happier and more resilient. If you're able to get out to some open space, see how you feel after some time outside.

Becky Dickinson

Contents

What is Resilience? 4

Why is Resilience So Important? 15

How Do We Become Resilient? 24

What's Stopping Me? 36

You've Got This! 42

Glossary 47

Index 48

The glossary

Some words in this book are in **bold**. When you read a **bold** word, think about what it means. If you don't know, you can look it up in the glossary at the end of the book.

What is Resilience?

We all have to face our own challenges in life – some small and some not so small. It could be learning how to multiply fractions, mastering that kickflip on your skateboard, or building the world's longest domino run. You may also have to deal with something really tough, like moving schools or bullying.

Dealing with emotional ups and downs is a part of life. We will all be confronted with worrying or upsetting situations from time to time, and it's completely normal to feel sad, stressed or anxious when this happens. The important thing is to pick ourselves up and keep going – and for that we need resilience.

A bouncing ball

Perhaps you've heard of resilience, but you aren't completely sure what it is. You might have heard your teacher talk about resilience, or something called a 'growth mindset'. (We'll get on to this on page 36!) Resilience helps us to overcome disappointment and recover from difficult situations.

If you drop a stone onto the floor, it stays there. But what happens if you drop a tennis ball onto the same floor? It bounces!

It's similar for people who are showing resilience. Resilience can help us to 'bounce back' from life's falls. It helps us to deal with challenges and move forward in a positive way.

Resilient objects and materials

Certain objects and materials can also be described as resilient. These materials aren't just strong: they can also tolerate shocks and stress. You can bend or twist objects made from resilient materials and they will return to their original shape and size. This means they can continue to function even in challenging or extreme conditions. Here are some examples:

Wool

As well as being soft and warm, the fleeces produced by sheep and other animals are surprisingly resilient. The wool fibres can be twisted more than 20 000 times without snapping. This means clothes made from wool will still fit you even after being stretched or squashed.

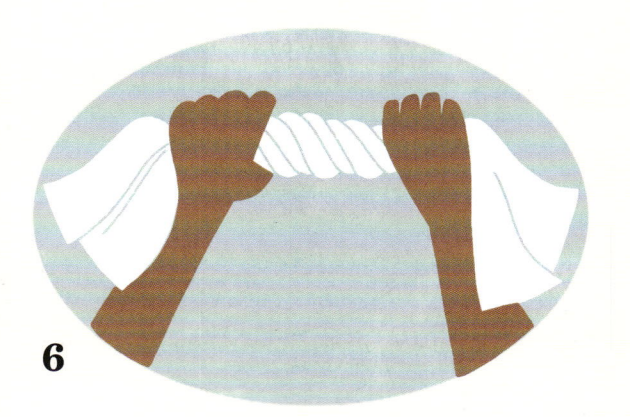

Titanium

Titanium is a strong, lightweight metal. It was named after the Titans, who were powerful Greek gods. As well as being extremely tough, titanium doesn't rust or get damaged easily, which makes it very resilient. Titanium is useful for making all sorts of items including tennis rackets, scissors, bicycle frames, watches, aeroplane wings and even artificial legs and hip joints.

Weeds

Have you ever noticed how weeds have a habit of growing anywhere and everywhere – especially where they're not wanted? They can survive frost and slugs, and can even grow through cracks in tough materials like concrete. Why? Because weeds are some of the most resilient plants on earth.

Coil springs

A coil spring is a curly metal spiral. You can stretch it out to make it longer or compress it to make it smaller, but when you stop stretching or compressing it, a spring will ping back to its original form. Which means a trampoline can stay springy, bounce ... after bounce ... after bounce ... after bounce!

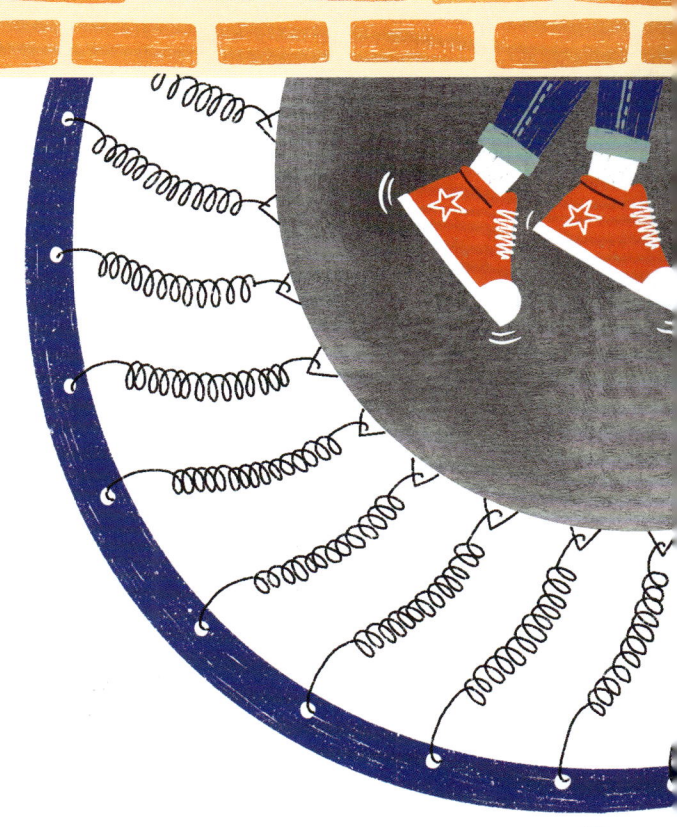

An ordinary superpower

If you could have any superpower, what would it be?

INVISIBILITY?

X-RAY VISION?

TIME TRAVEL?

SUPERHUMAN STRENGTH?

JETPACK FEET?

... Well, how about resilience?

Unlike other superpowers, resilience isn't something that only exists in films or your imagination. It's a superpower that can live inside all of us. It won't give you a magic cape or the ability to see through walls, but resilience will help you to overcome everyday obstacles like standing up to people who are mean, or give you the strength to ask for help when you're struggling with something. In fact, resilience might just be the only superpower you need!

As you read this book, you will discover how to become your own superhero. Each chapter contains resilience 'building blocks' that will help you become stronger on the inside. Each block represents a different quality or skill, and the more blocks you collect, the more resilient you will become.

As your pile of blocks grows, you will find it easier to face challenges and recover from difficult times. By the time you get to the last page, you will be ready to take on the world!

A secret strength

Close your eyes for a second and try to imagine an invisible, yet supremely powerful, muscle. Not a physical muscle, like biceps (the bulgy ones in arms) or quadriceps (the ones in thighs that help people run), or even muscles in the heart that you can't see from the outside. This imaginary inner muscle connects the mind and body. This is where your superpower starts.

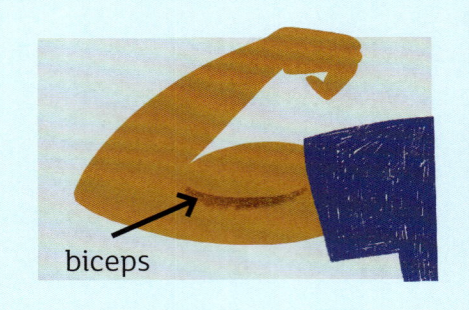

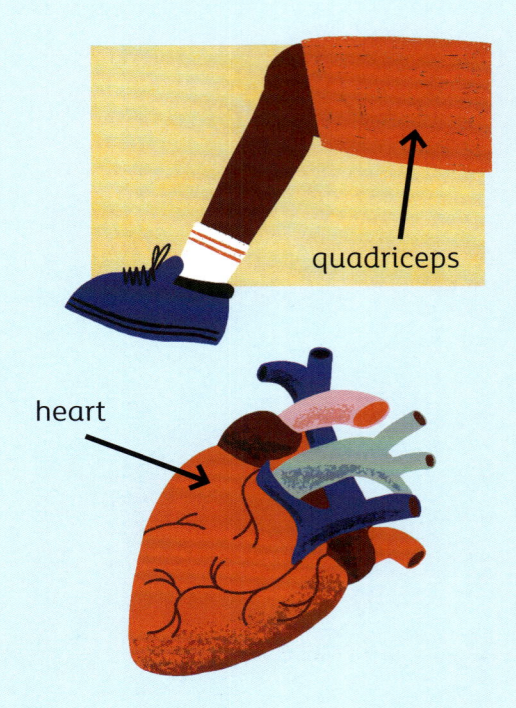

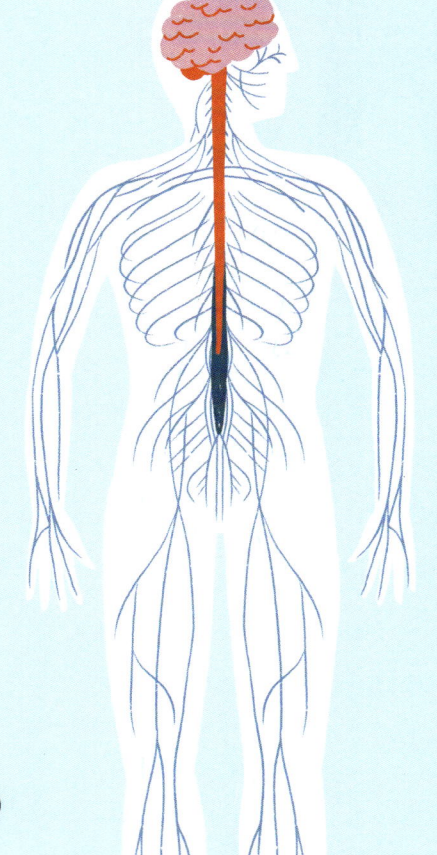

biceps

quadriceps

heart

Just as muscles make the body strong, resilience strengthens the mind. The more resilient you are, the less likely you are to give up or run out of energy when things go wrong. Resilience helps us to keep trying – and trying again – until we reach our goals.

Like any muscle, the brilliant thing about resilience is that the more you use it, the stronger it will become.

Remarkable role models

The world is full of people who have shown incredible resilience, even when faced with extreme challenges.

Helen Keller

Helen Keller became famous for campaigning for equal rights for women and disabled people. Born in America in 1880, Helen became blind and deaf after a serious illness when she was less than two years old. She found her situation frustrating, so she used her hands to communicate. Helen learned several ways to converse, including sign language and **Braille**, and worked really hard to make sure her speech was clear. She became the first deaf-blind person to achieve a university degree. Later, Helen wrote for newspapers and magazines on a variety of topics, as well as writing books about her experience. In the 1940s and 1950s, Helen travelled all over the world giving speeches.

> " ... although the world is full of suffering, it is full also of the overcoming of it."
> **Helen Keller**

Your own challenges might seem insignificant compared to other people's, but that doesn't mean they are not real. Everyone has their own struggles to deal with and they are all important.

What would you do?

Read the following scenarios and think about how you would react in each situation.

1. You've just spent three hours carefully constructing a model of a rainforest for school when your little brother comes along and sits on it. Do you:

  a. Sit on your little brother.

  b. Tell your teacher you were bitten by a poisonous centipede and couldn't complete your model.

  c. Feel really upset that your hard work has been spoiled. However, you know that staying angry won't help, so you decide to salvage as much as you can and use these bits to make a new and improved model.

2. You're about to meet your friends in the park when it starts raining. Do you:

  a. Decide not to go, then moan that you're bored.

  b. Demand to move to a country where it doesn't rain.

  c. Grab a waterproof jacket and go anyway. The rain won't last forever.

3. You haven't been picked for the basketball team, despite attending every practice. Do you:

a. Leave the club and give up playing basketball forever.

b. Pretend you didn't really want to be picked anyway.

c. Talk to your coach about how disappointed you feel, and ask how to increase your chances of being picked next time. Then practise more often to improve your skills.

How did you do?

If you picked mostly option c, well done! You have an attitude of resilience. A resilient person refuses to be defeated by setbacks and tries to find solutions to them instead.

If you picked option a or b for some of your answers, don't worry. It's completely natural to feel discouraged when things don't work out, especially when you've tried your best. Feeling upset about something shows that you care, which is a great reason not to give up.

As you start collecting resilience building blocks, you will find ways to turn disappointment into determination.

13

Resilience building blocks: part 1

Difficulties and challenges are part of life, but resilience helps us to stay strong and overcome disappointment. Resilient people stay positive when things go wrong and look for solutions to their problems. You can build resilience on a good foundation of:

- Determination
- Perseverance
- Courage
- Inner strength

When a situation is extremely difficult or upsetting, it's natural to feel distressed. It's important to acknowledge this and to share your feelings with a trusted adult so they can provide the comfort and support you need.

Why is Resilience So Important?

You might be wondering: what's the point of resilience? Why bother learning how to cope with **adversity**? Wouldn't it be better to just avoid problems in the first place? Unfortunately, we can't always choose what happens to us. Life can be a bit like a rollercoaster.

There are ups and downs, twists and turns. And once you get on, there's no getting off. The best thing is to hold on tight.

Your 'ups' might include going on holiday, celebrating your birthday or watching an **engrossing** film. Then there are the 'downs', like difficult tests at school, feeling ill, or your best friend moving away.

And then there are the things we could never have imagined …

Coronavirus and resilience

In 2019, a new type of coronavirus, which causes a disease called Covid-19, began infecting many people. It spread across the world.

Coronavirus brought enormous changes to most people's lives. Schools were closed, events were cancelled and many of us were unable to see friends and family for long periods of time. Sadly, some people also had to cope with the death of someone they loved.

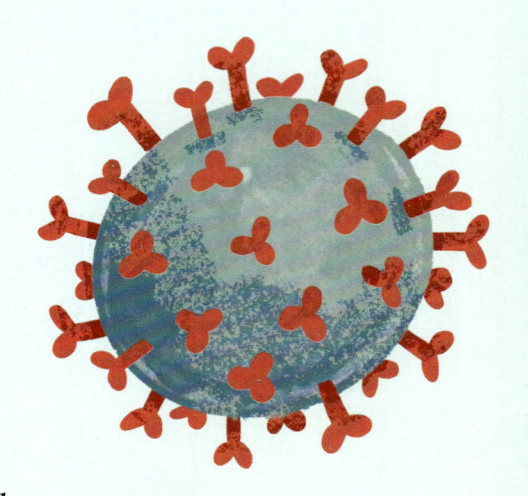

Although times have been very hard, coronavirus has also shown us how resilient we can be. Millions of children adapted to online learning, we found new ways of keeping fit and being creative in our own homes, and many of us were able to use technology to keep in contact with our loved ones so that we could all stay safe.

Thankfully, pandemics are rare, but there will always be events that we can't control. However, we can change the way we respond to them. And that's why resilience is so important: it doesn't make the bad stuff go away, but it does make difficult situations easier to deal with.

Remarkable role models

Bethany Hamilton

Bethany Hamilton was born in Hawaii in 1990 and fell in love with surfing as a child. But in 2003, when she was thirteen years old, her left arm was completely bitten off by a tiger shark. However, the resilient teenager refused to let the attack shatter her aspirations of becoming a professional surfer. Once her wound had healed, she conquered her fears and got back on her surfboard. Within two years, she won her first national surfing title and at seventeen years old, achieved her dream of surfing professionally. She went on to win numerous competitions. As well as being a successful professional surfer, Bethany runs courses to help other people fulfil their dreams.

"Courage doesn't mean you don't get afraid. Courage means you don't let fear stop you."
Bethany Hamilton

17

Mistakes are great

Nobody likes making mistakes, but they are part of life. Have you ever considered what would happen if you never made a mistake? You wouldn't learn as much!

Resilience gives us the courage to take risks without fear of failure. It can also boost our problem-solving skills by motivating us to look at why something didn't work out and try a different approach. This stops us from making the same mistakes repeatedly and helps us become better decision-makers.

Resilient people might not get the correct answer or achieve their goal the first time round – or even the fiftieth time – but they keep trying, and they don't let disappointment stop them. We need perseverance to keep working towards our goals, but it's resilience that gives us the strength to start again when things go wrong.

Remarkable role models

Thomas Alva Edison

Lewis Latimer

Thomas Alva Edison was a famous inventor who was born in America in 1847. He is best-known for developing the domestic light bulb and the electric power system to provide homes with electricity. But Thomas's first light bulb was not a success. In fact, it took him years to produce a light bulb that worked, proving that resilience is the path to success. He said: "Results! Why, man, I have gotten a lot of results! I know several thousand things that won't work."

Thomas's achievement wasn't just down to his own efforts, though. Another man, Lewis Latimer, improved the original light bulb design by making it more practical and affordable for ordinary households. Lewis was also born in America, just a year after Thomas, in 1848. His parents had escaped from slavery but it was a time of deep **racism**. Although Lewis was added to the National Inventors Hall of Fame for his work on bulb filaments, his race meant he didn't attract the same kind of attention as other **pioneers**. But it's thanks to his resilience that we can light up our homes today.

Be prepared

Achieving goals and learning new skills takes time and preparation. Here's a step-by-step guide to help you work towards a goal of your own.

Step 1. Choose a SMART goal

- **S**pecific – be precise. For example, instead of saying you want to get better at Maths, say you want to understand algebra or angles.
- **M**easurable – keep track of your progress so you know when you've achieved your goal. For example, every time you have an algebra test you could record your results so you can watch them improve.
- **A**chievable – is your goal realistic? You might need to start with smaller goals first.
- **R**elevant – your goal should be important to you.
- **T**imely – setting yourself a date by which you need to complete your goal helps you to stay motivated.

You might not be able to work towards your goal every day, and that's fine. Just do what you can when it's possible.

Step 2. Make a plan of action

Don't try to reach your goal in one go. Instead, break it down into smaller steps so it seems less daunting.

Ask yourself:

- What will be my first step?
- What should I do after that?
- What strengths do I have that will help me achieve my goal?
- Have I done anything similar before?

Tip: When you are learning new skills, make time for things you are good at. Reminding yourself of what you *can* do gives you confidence for tackling things you can't do yet.

Step 3. Be prepared for setbacks

Don't despair if you don't achieve your goals straight away. Failure can be a valuable opportunity to learn.

When you are struggling, ask yourself:

- What is getting in my way?
- How can I get around it?
- How can I stay positive?

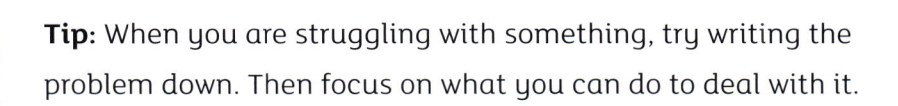

Tip: When you are struggling with something, try writing the problem down. Then focus on what you can do to deal with it.

Step 4. Rest and reflect

Taking a break from your goals helps you to renew your energy and allows you time to contemplate your progress. After a challenging situation, ask yourself:

- What went well?
- What could have gone better?
- What could I have done differently?
- Did I stay positive?
- What will I do next time?

Every time you use a plan like this to learn new skills, you build resilience! The next time you find yourself in a similar situation, you will find it easier to handle.

Tip: Imagine yourself achieving your goal. How do you feel? Visualizing yourself in the future can help you to keep going.

Remarkable role models

Chloe Morgan

Chloe Morgan loved football as a child. However, there weren't many women footballers on TV so she didn't think she could choose football as a career. Instead, inspired by the film *Erin Brockovich*, she decided to become a lawyer to help people. Chloe didn't know any lawyers so she sent off hundreds of requests for work experience to find out more about what they did. Her resilience paid off!

Chloe is now a full-time lawyer *and* a professional footballer. She does a lot of planning to make sure she has time for both her passions. During the day she works as a lawyer, then at weekends and in the evenings she's the goalkeeper for Crystal Palace F.C. Previously, Chloe played for Tottenham Hotspur, and the team got promoted to the FA Women's Super League. Chloe is also on the Women in Football board and has won awards for her part in making everyone feel welcome in football. In 2021, two major TV channels announced they would show women's football matches live on TV. Chloe was delighted.

> "I want change and I feel a sense of responsibility to try and get that change moving."
> **Chloe Morgan**

Resilience building blocks: part 2

Life would be boring if we never got anything wrong! In fact, failure often leads to success – but only if we don't give up. Here are some of the resilience building blocks we have accumulated in this chapter.

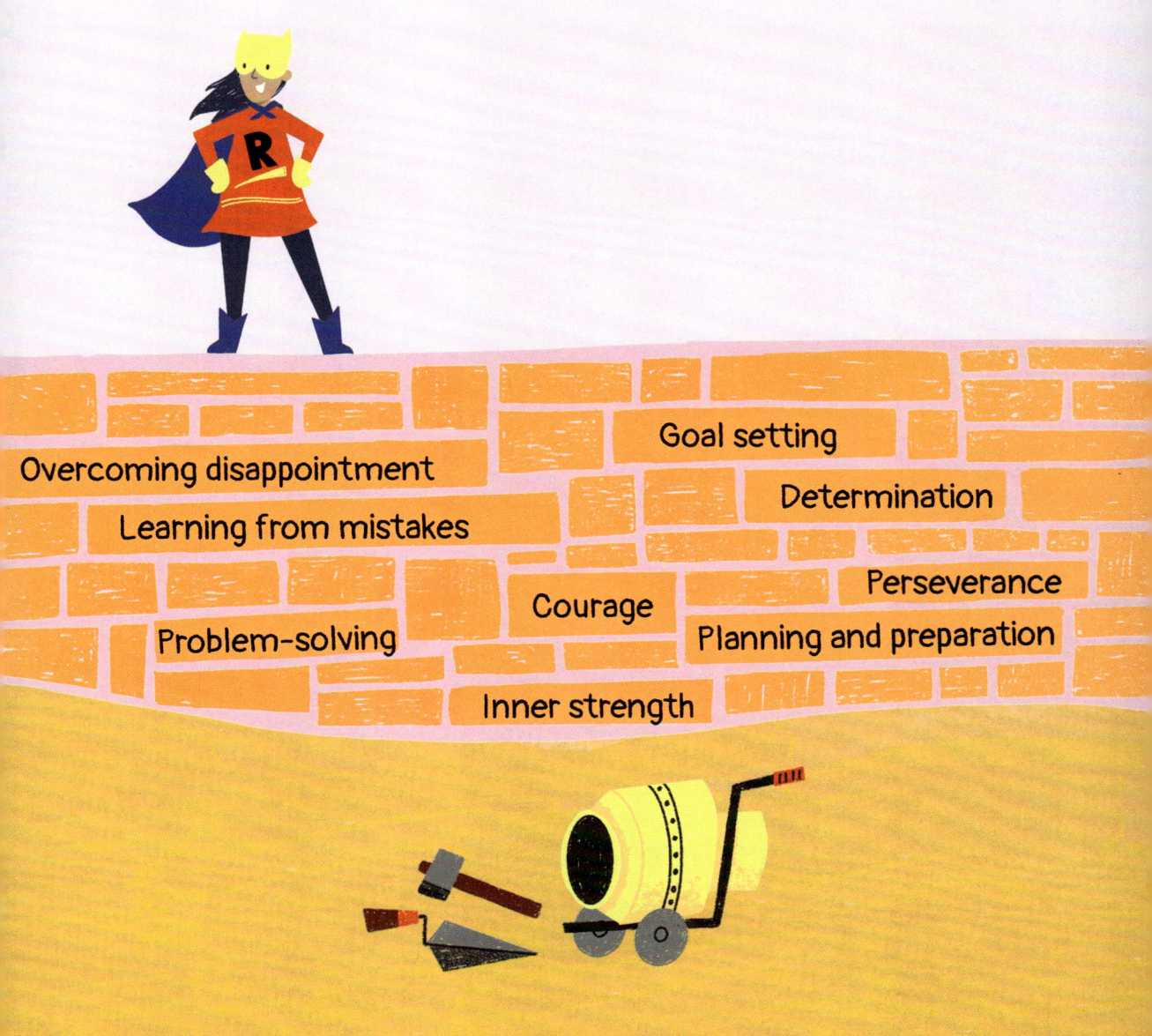

Overcoming disappointment

Goal setting

Learning from mistakes

Determination

Problem-solving

Courage

Perseverance

Planning and preparation

Inner strength

How Do We Become Resilient?

The **World Health Organisation** (WHO) says that health is made up of three things: physical, mental and social wellbeing.

For good physical health, you need to eat a balanced diet including plenty of fruit and vegetables, drink lots of water, exercise and sleep well.

Besides strengthening your heart and muscles, exercise causes your brain to release chemicals called endorphins, which make you feel good inside. So being active boosts your physical and mental health at the same time – that's a double boost for resilience!

Getting at least nine hours' sleep a night lets your body and brain recharge. As well as restoring your energy, sleep is also good for your concentration levels, your mood and your **immune system**, meaning you are less likely to get ill. And when you are healthy, focused and in good spirits, you are much more likely to be resilient.

Between school, homework, tests, tidying up, staying active, doing things you enjoy and keeping up with friends, life can be hectic at times. That's when you can start to feel stressed or overwhelmed, so it's important to make time to look after your mental, as well as your physical, health.

Your mental health affects your mood, and this can have a big impact on resilience. Just like not eating or sleeping properly reduces your physical energy, feeling stressed or worried can reduce your mental energy. This can make it harder to deal with problems. Learning how to stay calm and cope with difficult emotions is another important building block for becoming resilient.

Lots of people find that yoga is a good way to relax, or you could try practising mindfulness or meditation. These are techniques which help us to be in the moment rather than worrying about things that have happened in the past or might happen in the future. Turn the page to find out more about these relaxation techniques.

Ways to relax

Yoga

There's a lot more to yoga than stretching. The tradition of yoga started in India around 5000 years ago, and now exists in more than a hundred different forms, with a style to suit everyone. One popular form is called hatha yoga.

In Sanskrit, the word yoga means 'union'. Yoga can bring the mind and body into harmony through **poses**, deep breathing and meditation.

As well as relieving tension in your muscles, yoga can help you feel happier, more peaceful and more positive. Some poses require a lot of concentration and this trains your mind to become better at focusing. By practising yoga regularly, you can transfer these benefits to your daily life, helping you to feel mentally and physically stronger.

Meditation

Meditation is another centuries-old way of keeping calm. It can help clear your mind.

Although it is associated with **Buddhism** and other religions, you don't have to be religious to try it.

There are many ways to meditate. One option is to choose a word, known as a mantra, and repeat it inside your head. You could use a word like 'peace' or 'calm', or you can make one up.

Scientists have found that meditation can cause physical changes in the brain. Amazingly, it can increase the regions associated with learning, memory and controlling emotions, and decrease the amygdala (*say* uh-mig-duh-luh)– the part of the brain that plays a role in stress.

Mindfulness

Mindfulness is another mental exercise that's based on meditation. It helps you to focus on what's happening around you and draws your mind away from negative thoughts and worries.

One simple mindfulness exercise is to take a small object, such as an apple or a leaf, and give it your full attention for a few minutes. Really notice the way it looks, feels and smells.

You can be mindful in your daily life too – for example, when eating a meal or washing your hands. It's just about living in the moment. Yoga, meditation and mindfulness can all contribute to a happy, healthy brain, so they can be useful building blocks for developing resilience, too.

Tip: If you think you would like to try any of these techniques, ask an adult to help you to find a book, an app or a safe website to guide you. There may also be children's yoga classes at school or in your local area that you could join. Don't worry if you try them but they're not helpful for you. You might prefer to relax just by playing outside or reading a book and that's fine, too.

Take a breath

It sounds almost too simple to be true, but taking a few slow, deep breaths really can help you to feel calmer during moments of stress or anxiety. Often, these are the times when we need extra resilience.

When we feel worried, our brain thinks we are in danger, even when we're not. This triggers a surge of hormones, such as **adrenalin**, to be released into our bloodstream. This activates something called the **fight or flight** response, which prepares the body to react more quickly. As a result, our heart rate increases and we take fast, shallow breaths, which add to that stressed feeling. But we can cancel this reaction and calm our brain by taking a few slow, deep breaths.

Learn how to 'belly breathe'

This is a good technique to use whenever you are feeling anxious. Try to practise belly breathing when you are feeling calm, so you'll know how to do it when you really need it. You can practise when lying down, sitting or standing.

1. Find a comfortable position and place one hand on your belly.
2. Inhale slowly through your nose for four seconds. You should feel your belly expand like a balloon.
3. Exhale slowly through your mouth for four seconds, feeling your belly deflate.
4. Repeat a few times.

Stronger together

None of us can get through hard times without support. Having someone to turn to is one of the most important building blocks for resilience and overall wellbeing. However resilient we are, sometimes we need help to reach our goals or overcome challenges in our lives.

Imagine a football match. One team has the most skilful striker in the world, but the players don't pass to each other. The other team is made up of average players who all work together. Who do you think will win? The team who support each other, of course!

It can take courage to admit you're struggling with something, but asking for help isn't a sign of weakness; it's a sign of strength. Talk about your feelings with someone you trust, such as a grandparent, friend, or teacher. Sometimes just speaking about your worries can make them feel smaller.

Protecting yourself on the inside

Your self-esteem is the way you feel about your character and your abilities. This doesn't mean showing off or thinking you are better than others; it's about having respect for yourself and believing in your potential.

People with a strong sense of self-esteem have confidence in their own worth and their abilities, whereas people with low self-esteem might not think very highly of themselves and expect to fail when they try something new. They might think things like:

I'm boring. Nobody wants to play with me.

My friends' lives are much more exciting than mine.

I'll never be good at sport.

We all have days when we feel a bit gloomy or doubt our own abilities. It's important to feel our feelings, but not let them take over.

Having a strong sense of self-esteem is a key factor in building resilience because feeling secure about yourself helps you to approach challenges with confidence.

Imagine there's a school play coming up and you'd love to take part. If you say to yourself, *I might forget my lines, then people will laugh at me,* this negative thought will make you feel worried, so you might decide to avoid the audition. In other words, your thoughts will have controlled your actions.

However, if you say to yourself, *I'm brave and I work hard to remember my lines,* this positive thought will build your confidence and motivate you to go to the audition. With this mindset, your thoughts will have influenced your behaviour in a productive way.

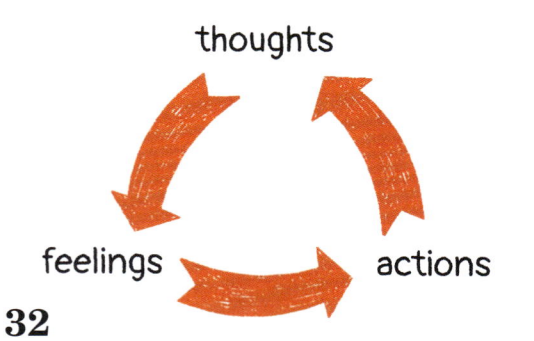

thoughts → actions → feelings → thoughts

Just as you nourish your body with nutritious food, you can nourish your sense of self-esteem with positive thoughts. Here are some tools that can help:

- Listen to the way you talk to yourself in your own head. Is your inner voice kind or mean? Would you speak to a friend that way? If not, you shouldn't speak to yourself that way either.

- Stop comparing yourself to other people.

- Celebrate the qualities, talents and characteristics that make you special and unique.

- Imagine you have an invisible best friend who sits on your shoulder and whispers words of encouragement into your ear. (Don't worry, no one else has to know they're there!)

Tip: If you find it hard to identify your best qualities, you could ask someone who knows you well for their opinion. It's not just about being successful at school or sport; special characteristics also include things like being thoughtful or being a supportive friend.

Remarkable role models

Ade Adepitan

Ade Adepitan is a well-known television presenter and former athlete. Born in Nigeria in 1973, Ade was just a baby when he became ill with polio. This disease meant he couldn't use his legs in the same way as before.

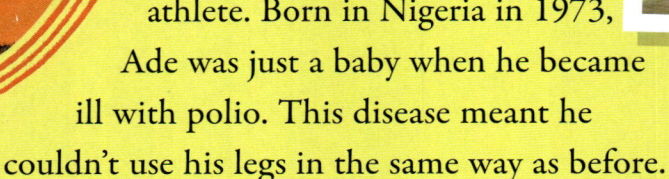

Ade moved to the UK in 1976. He wore **calipers** to help him walk, and these also helped him play football with his friends. When Ade started to use a wheelchair, he could move around much more quickly and decided to try another sport. He began wheelchair basketball training six hours a day, six days a week, and dreamed of playing for Great Britain. His hard work paid off and he was selected for the Paralympic team. During his career, Ade won many medals including bronze at the 2004 Paralympics in Athens and gold at the Paralympic World Cup in Manchester in 2005.

"Three words I'd use to describe myself are thoughtful, ambitious and determined."
Ade Adepitan, in an interview for a BBC blog, 2012

Resilience building blocks: part 3

By putting the information you have read so far into practice, you will be well on your way to becoming even more resilient. Let's have a look at some of the new building blocks you can now add to your collection.

- Nurturing your self-esteem
- Having positive thoughts
- Eating nutritious food
- Getting enough sleep
- Using relaxation techniques
- Asking for help
- Staying active
- Goal setting
- Overcoming disappointment
- Determination
- Learning from mistakes
- Perseverance
- Courage
- Problem-solving
- Planning and preparation
- Inner strength

What's Stopping Me?

Some people appear to be very confident. But the truth is no one is born a great runner, or a super swimmer, or able to speak multiple languages. We all have to work at these things, but sometimes we can be intimidated by other people's achievements.

So, what enables some people to pursue their goals but stops others from starting to try? It all comes down to the beliefs we hold about ourselves and the world. We call this our mindset. There are two different types of mindset, but one is more helpful than the other for developing resilience.

Fixed mindset

I'd love to roller-skate but there's no way I could do that.

Growth mindset

If I keep practising, I'll improve. This is great!

There are some things you can't change about yourself, such as your height or the colour of your eyes. These features are determined by your **DNA**. But there are other things you can change, such as whether you can play the drums or calculate percentages.

You might not become a musician or a mathematician overnight. But you can take your first steps towards your goals by developing a growth mindset. People who have a growth mindset believe they can improve their abilities through practice or by trying a different approach.

The opposite of a growth mindset is a fixed mindset. This is when you think you can't change your abilities so there's little point in trying. This might be because you've struggled with a subject in the past or haven't had the right support. Fortunately, there are lots of ways to change your mindset.

> Having a growth mindset is a brilliant way to boost your resilience, because believing you can get better at something motivates you to keep going, even when it's tricky.

37

Your plastic-fantastic brain

Scientists have demonstrated that the brain is like a muscle: it changes and gets stronger the more you use it. This means we can learn new skills and improve our abilities.

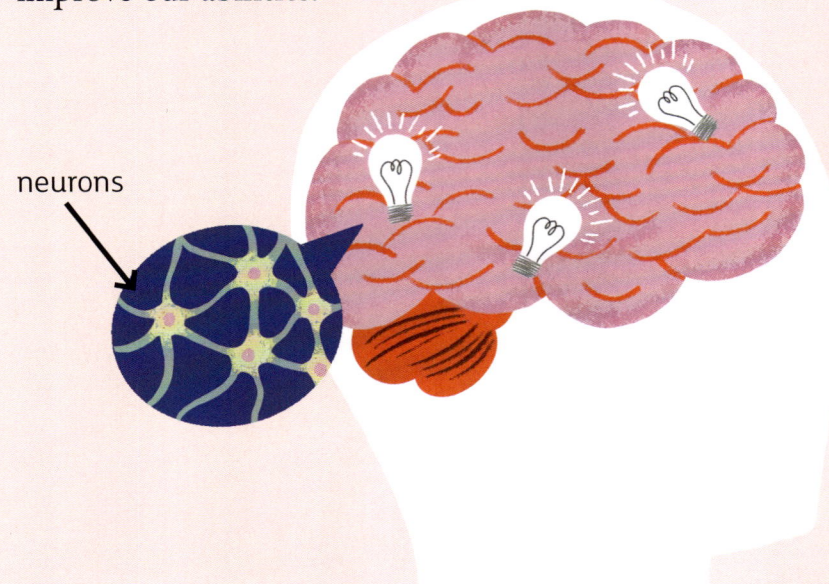

neurons

Your brain contains billions of tiny nerve cells called neurons. These cells are connected to one another by a network of microscopic branches, a bit like an incredibly intricate cobweb. The connections allow the neurons to communicate with each other, which is how we are able to think and solve problems.

When you learn new things, these connections multiply and get stronger. In fact, the more you challenge yourself, the stronger they become. We call this brain plasticity, or neuroplasticity.

Understanding this can inspire you to adopt a growth mindset because it proves that practice really does make a difference. So having a growth mindset is a keystone of resilience.

More brainy facts

If you lined up all the neurons in your brain, they would stretch 1000 kilometres.

Neurons are tiny – you could fit more than 30 000 of them onto the head of a pin!

Scientists used special imaging technology to show that memorizing thousands of streets had caused part of London taxi drivers' brains to grow. You can't say that about a satnav!

Brain information can travel at an incredible 431 kilometres per hour. That's faster than a Formula 1 racing car.

Researchers studied the brain of scientist Albert Einstein after his death. They found that the **density** of neurons in Einstein's brain was greater than average. That's some growth mindset!

Developing a growth mindset

Whatever you want to achieve, it all starts with believing you can do it. Once you realize that your brain is **malleable**, there is nothing stopping you from learning new activities, skills or languages – and being brilliant at them!

Here are some tips that can help you build a growth mindset.

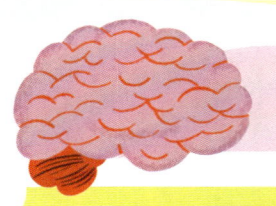

Growth mindset

- Move out of your comfort zone – whether it's following a recipe for the first time, or tackling a tricky puzzle, challenges help our brains to grow.

- Focus on effort not results – some of our best learning happens when we get something wrong because it gives us the opportunity to learn from our mistakes.

- Try different strategies – we all learn in different ways, so if one method doesn't work for you, try another approach.

- Change 'not' into 'not yet' – if you are struggling to succeed at something, tell yourself you just haven't grasped it *yet*.

- Be patient - it takes lots of time and effort to learn a new skill, so keep persevering.

Always ask for help if you need it. Being resilient doesn't mean you have to cope with challenges alone.

Resilience building blocks: part 4

Science can help us to understand the way our brains work. We can use this evidence to continue building resilience.

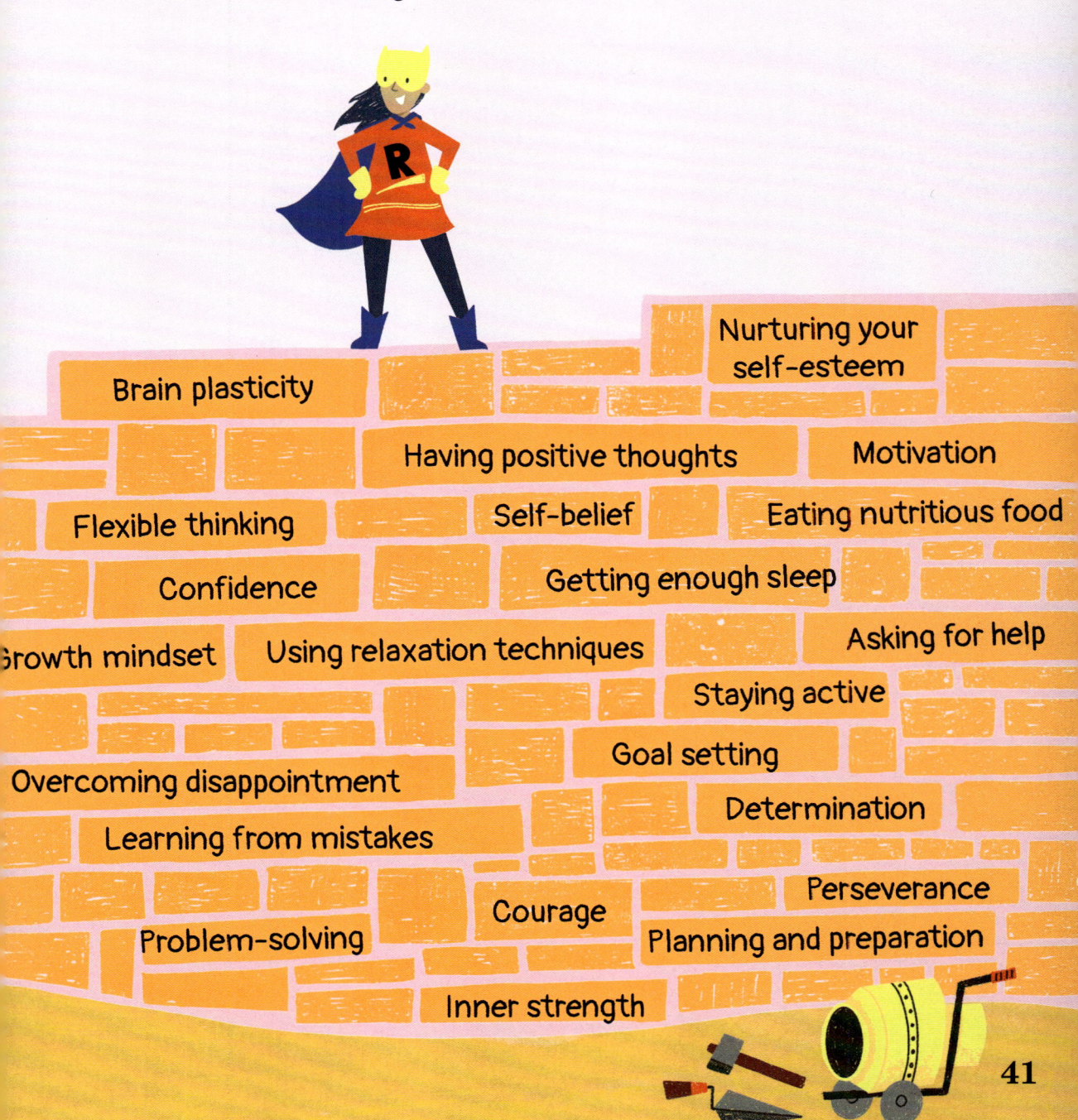

- Nurturing your self-esteem
- Brain plasticity
- Having positive thoughts
- Motivation
- Flexible thinking
- Self-belief
- Eating nutritious food
- Confidence
- Getting enough sleep
- Growth mindset
- Using relaxation techniques
- Asking for help
- Staying active
- Goal setting
- Overcoming disappointment
- Determination
- Learning from mistakes
- Perseverance
- Courage
- Planning and preparation
- Problem-solving
- Inner strength

You've Got This!

Every day, your brain juggles an astonishing number of thoughts. However, our brains are naturally designed to pay more attention to negative thoughts than positive ones. Thousands of years ago, this would have helped our ancestors stay alive by alerting them to dangers in the environment, such as predators prowling nearby while they hunted for food. As we have evolved, we no longer have to worry about being chased by fearsome predators, but our brains are still programmed to focus on negative thoughts.

Be positive

Thankfully, we can train our brains to be more optimistic and positive. This doesn't mean pretending that everything is OK when it isn't, or thinking you should be happy all of the time. Having a positive outlook is about noticing the good in situations, instead of finding things to complain about. Like resilience, positivity is a quality that can be practised and developed by everyone. As well as improving our own lives, positivity helps makes the world a better place, because positive people spread positivity, and that means everyone benefits!

So, what went well today? I'll go first: I'm glad I could catch up with a friend for a walk at lunchtime.

I practised playing the guitar. It's hard work, but I'm definitely improving!

My class went litter-picking and I liked seeing what a difference we made to the park.

"You may not control all the events that happen to you, but you can decide not to be reduced by them."
Dr Maya Angelou, author and poet, from her book *Letter to My Daughter*

Do the things you love

Whether it's caring for pets, building model sculptures or playing an instrument, it's really important to make time for the things you enjoy. Concentrating on a favourite activity helps you to switch off from niggling worries and feel focused and happy. Scientists call this being in a 'state of flow' and it's a great way to boost positivity.

Having a positive attitude is one of the most important ingredients for developing resilience. It helps us to feel confident, valued, and secure within our communities, society, and the wider world. What's more, being positive makes you more resilient and being resilient makes you feel positive. It's a win-win situation!

There are occasions when staying positive seems impossible. If you feel like this, it's essential to tell someone how you are feeling and to ask for help.

You

You are probably already more resilient than you realize. Try to think of a challenging situation you have already experienced. It doesn't matter what it was, as long as it felt significant to you. Now ask yourself:

How did I cope? (Remember that asking for help is a way of coping, too.)

How do I feel about it now?

What did I learn from the experience?

It's easy to forget to look back and think about how we got through tough times. But if you hold onto the things you have learned in this book on days when you feel anxious or disheartened, you will be ready for any challenges in the future.

You are a resilience superhero!

Now you know there are many brilliant skills and qualities associated with being resilient. Here are the ones you've collected while reading this book. Perhaps you can think of some more.

- Optimism
- Positivity
- Nurturing your self-esteem
- Brain plasticity
- Having positive thoughts
- Motivation
- Flexible thinking
- Self-belief
- Eating nutritious food
- Confidence
- Getting enough sleep
- Growth mindset
- Using relaxation techniques
- Asking for help
- Staying active
- Goal setting
- Overcoming disappointment
- Determination
- Learning from mistakes
- Perseverance
- Courage
- Problem-solving
- Planning and preparation
- Inner strength

Glossary

adrenalin: a hormone the body produces to prepare muscles for activity

adversity: a difficult or unpleasant situation

Braille: a system of raised dots that are read by feeling with the fingertips

Buddhism: a religion based on the teaching of Buddha

calipers: metal supports for someone's legs

density: how heavy or light an object is in relation to its size, or how compact it is

DNA: the chemical that carries genetic information for all living things

engrossing: interesting

fight or flight: the biological response to a threatening situation which prepares the body to either fight or run away

immune system: the system in the body that produces substances to protect against infection and disease

malleable: able to move without breaking

pioneers: the first people to do something

perseverance: being able to go on doing something even though it is difficult

poses: the positions in which someone holds their body in yoga

racism: any behaviour that assumes a person is not as good as someone else, because of their skin colour or race; this could be obvious like refusing to sit with someone – or it might be more subtle like making fun of someone's accent or stereotyping (for instance, saying one group of people all act in the same way)

World Health Organisation (WHO): an agency that works to protect the health of people all around the globe

Index

active 24–25, 35, 41, 46
Adepitan, Ade 34
Angelou, Maya 43
brain plasticity 38, 41
confidence 20, 41, 46
coronavirus 16
courage 14, 17–18, 23, 30, 35, 41, 46
determination 13–14, 23, 35, 41, 46
Edison, Thomas Alva 19
food 33, 35, 41–42, 46
Hamilton, Bethany 17
Keller, Helen 11
Latimer, Lewis 19
mindset 5, 32, 36–41, 46
Morgan, Chloe 22
perseverance 14, 18, 23, 35, 41, 46–47
positivity 43–44, 46
relaxation 25, 26–27, 35, 41, 46
self-esteem 31, 32–33, 35, 41, 46
sleep 24–25, 35, 41, 46
SMART 20
strength 8–10, 14, 18, 20, 23, 30, 35, 41, 46
superpower 8–9, 10